21st
Century
Skills Library

COOL CAREERS

ENVIRONMENTALIST

TAMRA B. ORR

Published in the United States of America by
Cherry Lake Publishing, Ann Arbor, Michigan
www.cherrylakepublishing.com

Content Adviser
Thomas Pypker, PhD, Assistant Professor, School of Forest Resources and
Environmental Science, Michigan Technological University

Credits
Photos: Cover and page 1, ©Mark Boulton/Alamy; page 4, ©Edward Parker/Alamy;
page 6, ©Roberto Soncin Gerometta/Alamy; page 8, ©David Roos, used under
license from Shutterstock, Inc.; page 10, ©INTERFOTO Pressebildagentur/Alamy;
page 11, ©Deserttrends/Dreamstime.com; page 12, ©Sylvia Cordaiy Photo Library
Ltd/Alamy; page 14, ©AP Photo/Basil Childers; page 17, ©Tomochka, used under
license from Shutterstock, Inc.; page 18, ©ALIKI SAPOUNTZI/aliki image library/
Alamy; page 20, ©Marcin Balcerzak, used under license from Shutterstock, Inc.;
page 23, ©Anetta/Dreamstime.com; page 24, ©Larry Geddis/Alamy; page 26,
©kkaplin, used under license from Shutterstock, Inc.; page 27, ©Jim West/Alamy

Library of Congress Cataloging-in-Publication Data
Orr, Tamra B.
  Environmentalist / by Tamra B. Orr.
    p. cm.—(Cool careers)
  Includes index.
  ISBN-13: 978-1-60279-501-3
  ISBN-10: 1-60279-501-0
  1. Environmentalists—Juvenile literature. 2. Environmentalism—Juvenile literature.
I. Title. II. Series.
  GE80.O77 2010
  363.70023—dc22   2008047263

Cherry Lake Publishing would like to acknowledge
the work of The Partnership for 21st Century Skills.
Please visit *www.21stcenturyskills.org* for more information.

COOL CAREERS

TABLE OF CONTENTS

CHAPTER ONE
GUARDIANS OF THE PLANET

Natural disasters happen all the time. A hurricane blows in from the ocean. A tornado sweeps across acres of cornfields. Floods break concrete and sand barriers. Earthquakes rattle buildings. Mother Nature is powerful—and keeps reminding us of it, too.

A group of environmental workers clean oil from a beach after an oil spill in Wales.

Environmental disasters happen often as well. Unlike twisters and quakes, however, environmental disasters are caused by people. Oil spills into the ocean, killing all types of marine life. Nuclear power plants have emergencies that threaten everyone and everything in a huge area. Dangerous chemicals are released into the air or into the water. The list goes on and on.

LEARNING & INNOVATION SKILLS

In 1989, an oil tanker called the *Exxon Valdez* ran aground. It spilled more than 10 million gallons (38 million liters) of oil into Alaska's Prince William Sound. Thousands of seabirds, sea otters, harbor seals, bald eagles, killer whales, and salmon were killed. Massive cleanup efforts were made, but for many it was too late. Ten years after the spill, only two species had fully recovered. Shoreline habitats still show the effects 20 years after the spill.

What do you think could be done to prevent another accident like this one? Do you think it is possible to prevent all accidents that harm the environment? Why or why not?

In a natural disaster, the Red Cross, the Federal Emergency Management Agency, and other organizations are called in. Who gets a frantic phone call when a man-made disaster occurs? Many times, it is an environmentalist. He or she is the person who quickly understands what the threat is and what it will affect. Environmentalists know what must be done right away to save as many lives as possible.

Environmentalists are the guardians of the planet. They are taught how to protect the land, water, and air in many different

Theodore Roosevelt's idea to create Crater Lake National Park and other national parks was an important step in conserving land in the United States.

ways. They are the heroes who come in to help clean up the mess. They work to make sure it doesn't happen again.

21ˢᵀ CENTURY CONTENT

After the assassination of President William McKinley in 1901, Vice President Theodore Roosevelt suddenly became leader of the nation. He served the remaining three years of McKinley's term, and was reelected in 1904.

Roosevelt did many good things for the country. It was his interest in the environment, however, that made him one of our most respected leaders. During his time in office, he established the United States' first national park in Crater Lake, Oregon. He then created 4 more national parks and 51 wildlife refuges. He turned 150 million acres (61 million hectares) of forest into protected land. Roosevelt is considered by many to be a true environmental hero.

An environmentalist is a person who works to protect the planet. People have been doing this for centuries. Air pollution has been around since before factories and automobiles were invented. It came from dust, wood smoke, **tanneries**, and animal manure. As far back as ancient times, people had to cope with water pollution from **sewage**.

During the 18th century, Benjamin Franklin fought against water pollution. He knew that tar from coal production dripped into rivers. He also knew that rubber plants poured dangerous chemicals into streams. Coal smoke filled the air in larger cities. By the 19th century, smog was so bad that, in London, people began to die from polluted air. Terrible **epidemics** that killed many people were linked to water pollution.

As the 20th century began, industries grew and environmental problems continued to get worse. In New York and

The smog in the city of Shanghai, China,
is easy to see during sunset.

Los Angeles, air pollution was so bad that people were dying. The National Coast Anti-Pollution League was formed in 1922 to stop the dumping of oil into water. In 1955, the first international air pollution conference was held. Soon after this conference, Rachel Carson's book *Silent Spring* told readers all over the world about the dangers of pesticides. Then in 1969, the Cuyahoga River in Cleveland, Ohio, caught fire from the oil and chemicals that were in it.

21ST CENTURY CONTENT

In 1986, in the Ukraine, operators at the Chernobyl nuclear power plant ran a test on one of the **reactors**. Through a series of human mistakes and mechanical errors, there was a huge power surge. Next came explosions and fires. The reactor was completely destroyed. Massive amounts of **radioactive** materials were released and spread over Europe. Countless people were exposed. Since the accident, many people have died from radiation-related cancers. It was a global wake-up call that nuclear power plants could be extremely dangerous.

Environmentalists fought against this destruction of the world's water, land, and air. In 1970, the Environmental Protection Agency was formed. It is a federal agency that watches out for the health of the planet. Cars were altered so they would pollute the air less. Sewage treatment plants helped clean up the nation's rivers.

The city of Cleveland, Ohio, is on the banks of the Cuyahoga River. At one time, the river was so polluted it caught fire.

Unless something is done, more trash will continue to pile up in landfills every day.

The world, however, continues to face huge environmental problems. Today, issues such as global climate change and overflowing **landfills** are growing concerns. Though these problems exist, better choices are being made, and everyone is learning that Earth is our only home. We must treat it well.

CHAPTER TWO
ON THE JOB

It was the moment that Dr. David E. Guggenheim had dreamed of ever since he was a little boy. He had wanted to be a submarine pilot for as long as he could remember. Now, he was going to get the chance. Guggenheim was on an expedition

Greenpeace works to preserve the environment. The organization employs many different enviomentalists.

in the middle of the Bering Sea. The expedition was led by members of an organization known as Greenpeace. Its members are dedicated to protecting the environment. The team was there to log the sea corals they found at depths of up to 2,000 feet (610 meters). Everyone on the boat had just put their names into a coffee mug. The person whose name was drawn would get the chance to pilot the single-person **submersible**. Guggenheim's name was chosen.

"It was completely dark and cold," he says. "Then I turned on the lights—and the world exploded with color. The first thing I saw was an octopus walking along through the water. I thought, 'Mine are the first human eyes to see this place and this moment.' I felt small and humble and I was reminded of how important it is to keep exploring our world."

Known as the Ocean Doctor, Guggenheim is no stranger to water. He is a marine biologist and has spent much of his life trying to make the world's oceans healthier, cleaner places. He fell in love with the sea when he was small, fishing with his father in New Jersey. "I was a teenager when I first went under the water," Guggenheim recalls. "I asked for scuba diving lessons for my fifteenth birthday. I went to the Florida Keys and was dropped in 35 feet of water." What he saw there amazed him: colorful fish, bright coral, and a whole world he hadn't realized existed. "I said to myself, 'this is what I want to do.' It was a wonderful feeling to find such mysteries to explore."

After leaving the Bering Sea, Guggenheim went to Cuba to explore and protect unknown parts of the Gulf of Mexico. "The joy of exploration and discovery is what the human mind is best at," he says. "We were designed to ask 'why?' and then search out the answers."

Christopher Swain's swims are impressive, but the real reason they are important is that they cause people to think carefully about water pollution.

Environmentalist Christopher Swain has experienced boat collisions, lightning storms, eel attacks, and toxic algae. He has also swum through water filled with nuclear waste. He does it to raise awareness of the importance of clean water and for his two daughters. He wants them to inherit a healthier world. As he says, "We live on a water planet. If we want to live healthy lives, we need to go the distance to protect and restore the waters that we all depend on."

On July 1, 2003, Swain became the first person in history to swim the Columbia River. It runs through 1,243 miles (2,000 kilometers) of the Pacific Northwest. The trip was turned into an award-winning documentary called *Source to Sea: The Columbia River Swim.*

A year later, he made history again when he completed a 315-mile (507-km) swim of the Hudson River. This swim was captured on film in *Swim for the River.* Next came swims of Lake Champlain in New York and Vermont, and the Charles River in Massachusetts. All were done as part of a United Nations (UN) project.

Over the next four years, Swain continued to fight for the environment. In 2009, he plans on making an 800-mile (1,287-km) swim from Boston to Washington, D.C. He continues to work with the UN and has begun a campaign to recycle 1 billion pounds (454 million kg) of used electronics. Electronic devices are full of toxic chemicals and heavy metals. These chemicals hurt the environment. "High levels of heavy metals and dangerous chemicals aren't just affecting human health," he explains. "They are affecting ocean life as well: dolphins and whales routinely show dangerous levels of man-made toxins."

As environmentalists, Dr. David E. Guggenheim and Christopher Swain use their skills to make the world a better place.

LEARNING & INNOVATION SKILLS

Imagine that you have been given the chance to speak to the United Nations about the most pressing environmental problem in today's world. Which problem would you choose? How would you raise awareness of this problem? What skills would you need to raise awareness?

One reason environmentalists are working so hard to keep our water clean is to protect animals such as dolphins from being harmed by our waste.

CHAPTER THREE
SAVE THE WORLD TODAY!

S aving the world is a great goal to have, but becoming a superhero is a little difficult. Maybe you should become an environmentalist instead. You may not be able to

An environmental scientist examines samples from a pond in Scotland.

save hundreds of citizens at once, but you can make the planet cleaner. How many lives might that affect?

Becoming an environmentalist takes special training and education. One type of environmentalist is an environmental scientist. Environmental scientists often study how chemicals affect plants, animals, and people. They figure out what is in the air, water, and soil to determine how safe it is. Environmental scientists also give advice on how to clean up pollution. They recommend ways to better manage the land's resources. They help create laws to protect land, air, and water, and they work to make sure that everyone follows those laws. Most environmental scientists work in labs and offices. Others work outside, taking measurements, gathering samples, and conducting experiments.

Another type of environmentalist is an environmental engineer. These environmentalists find solutions to problems such as water and air pollution. They work to overcome the effects of **acid rain**, global climate change, and **ozone depletion**. Environmental engineers use biology and chemistry to learn how dangerous a problem might be. Then they offer advice on how to deal with the problem. Finally, they help to develop regulations to prevent other similar problems. Often, an engineer will give advice on how to best use the land or how to construct a building.

Some environmentalists are hydrologists. Hydrologists study water in the air, on Earth's surface, and underground.

They trace water's movement through the earth and the sky. They look at how fast water soaks through the soil. They also study the elements found in water and issues such as flood control.

Other environmentalists study design, economics, law, and management. No matter which type of environmentalist you want to be, you will need the following qualities:

Not all environmentalists are scientists. Environmental lawyers work to ensure that there are laws to help protect the environment.

- a passion for water, air, and land
- an interest in math, science, and computer science
- strong speaking and writing skills
- an ability to deal with severe weather
- an ability to work well alone or with a team
- an enjoyment of travel
- a willingness to ride in helicopters, trucks, and other vehicles

LIFE & CAREER SKILLS

Students who want to learn more about environmental careers often attend EcoCamp in Watkinsville, Georgia. At EcoCamp, students learn about solar power, organic gardening, and endangered plants. Recent EcoCamp projects have included building a wind turbine, geothermal earth tubes, and a hybrid vehicle. Wind turbines use the wind to make electricity. Geothermal earth tubes use the natural warmth of the ground to heat homes. Hybrid vehicles are powered by electricity and gas, making them more fuel efficient. Check out www.world.org for more information.

LIFE & CAREER SKILLS

In 2006, filmmaker Davis Guggenheim worked with former Vice President Al Gore to create a film called *An Inconvenient Truth*. Guggenheim had previously worked mostly on television dramas. Gore is a politician. Though they have very different backgrounds, they were able to work together to create a film that shares important knowledge about global climate changes. The film had a major impact. Millions of people flocked to theaters to see it.

Guggenheim and Gore prove that environmentalists can be found in almost any kind of career field. Even people with jobs not normally related to the environment can work to help spread information about environmental issues.

Most environmentalists have a college degree. Many earn a degree in environmental science. Environmentalists take classes in sciences such as biology and chemistry. They also take classes in politics, **conservation** and land use, economics, and public policy. These courses are needed because environmentalists often help write new environmental

Most environmentalists take at least some science classes in school.

legislation. Environmentalists must understand the law to fight for their cause. Dr. David E. Guggenheim says, "You need a unique set of skills. Knowing the science of it all lays the foundation, but you also have to know how to communicate well in order to speak to people's hearts. First you touch their emotions, and then you can make the intellectual argument."

CHAPTER FOUR
ON INTO THE FUTURE

As long as there are people, there will be environmental problems. As long as these problems exist, there will be a need for environmentalists to help solve them.

Thanks to the work of environmentalists, many people have learned to separate the recyclable items from the rest of their garbage.

Although we are getting better at taking care of the planet, we still have a long way to go. Fortunately, people are becoming more aware of environmental problems. They are more willing to do what is necessary to make a difference for the planet. For example, when recycling was first introduced, it was hard to get people to cooperate. They did not want to separate things such as newspapers and plastics from the rest of their garbage. Today, however, many people recycle. Curbside recycling programs have sprung up throughout the country.

LIFE & CAREER SKILLS

Do you know people who don't recycle used paper, plastic, and glass? Maybe you can put your leadership skills to work and convince them to start recycling. Start a recycling club at school or in your neighborhood. Talk to people about the importance of taking care of the planet. Volunteer to help them learn more about which items can be recycled. You don't have to wait until you are out of college and have a job to start taking care of the environment.

Experts predict that environmental jobs will increase by 25 percent between now and 2016. That is much faster than many other types of jobs. One reason for this increase is that companies must follow more environmental laws. They need employees who understand these laws.

Over the years, environmental issues have changed. Some problems are solved. Some are growing worse. In a recent survey, climate change was the number-one concern for

If you find yourself thinking about ways to fix global climate change, then you might have a future as an environmentalist.

Do you want to be an environmentalist? You can start now by volunteering to help keep your community clean.

Americans. Many environmentalists will focus on the problems caused by global climate change in the coming years. Global climate change can result in several serious problems. These include an increase in hurricanes, droughts, and heat waves. Maybe worst of all, climate change is beginning to melt the polar ice caps. As they melt, sea levels will rise. The oceans' delicate balance of life will be disturbed. The freshwater from the ice caps will mix with the oceans' salt water. This mixing may cause a change in ocean currents and interfere with many different life-forms.

LEARNING & INNOVATION SKILLS

Overpopulation is truly a global problem. Each day, more than 200,000 people are born. Imagine you were asked to develop a plan to address this issue. What changes would you want to make? What do you think would work? What would not?

Overpopulation is another continuing worry. Every year, more than 80 million people are added to the planet. As our population grows, the strain on the world's resources also grows. This increases the risk of more environmental problems.

Genetically modified food is another concern. This kind of food has had its **DNA** changed. This is done to protect food crops against diseases and poisons used to kill pests. It makes plants grow stronger and more quickly. Genetically modified food lasts longer and costs less in the store. The safety of this food, however, is still being debated.

The world will keep changing and so will problems with Earth's land, water, and air. As the planet changes, environmentalists will change as well. They will learn how to address new problems and find new approaches to old ones.

SOME FAMOUS ENVIRONMENTALISTS

Rachel Carson (1907–1964) is called the Mother of Modern Environmentalism. She was a nature writer who, through her research and books, pointed out the threat that pesticides pose to the environment. She was chief editor of the U.S. Fish and Wildlife Service publications and the author of the groundbreaking book *Silent Spring*.

Julia Butterfly Hill (1974–) is known as the Ancient Tree Saver. She lived in the branches of a 1,000-year-old redwood tree named Luna for 2 years to keep it from being cut down by loggers. She wrote a book about her experiences, and travels the world speaking about the importance of protecting the world's forests.

Robert F. Kennedy, Jr. (1954–) is an attorney who specializes in environmental law and works with organizations such as Riverkeeper and the Natural Resources Defense Council. He is a law professor at Pace University and supervises law students at the Environmental Litigation Clinic. He is the author of *The Riverkeepers* and many other books and articles.

Farley Mowat (1921–) is an environmentalist and author. He has written about the impact people have on traditional cultures and the environment. He spent years studying wolves in the Arctic and is the author of 14 adult books and five young-adult books about his research.

John Muir (1838–1914) is often called the Father of Our National Parks. Founder of the Sierra Club, he was passionate about the beauty of nature and equally passionate about protecting it. His writings influenced many people and contributed to the creation of national parks.

GLOSSARY

acid rain (ASS-id RAYN) rain that is polluted with gases from car engines and coal-burning power plants that damages the environment

conservation (kon-sur-VAY-shuhn) the prevention of waste or loss

DNA (dee-en-AY) molecules that carry the code that gives living things their special characteristics

epidemics (ep-i-DEM-iks) diseases affecting many people at the same time

genetically modified food (gen-NE-tik-lee MOD-ah-fide FOOD) food that has had its DNA artificially altered

landfills (LAND-filz) places where trash is buried between layers of dirt

ozone depletion (OH-zone dee-PLEE-shun) a steady decline in the amount of ozone, a gas that is a form of oxygen, in Earth's atmosphere

radioactive (rey-dee-oh-AK-tiv) made up of atoms that break down and give off harmful rays

reactors (ree-ACT-orz) buildings where nuclear reactions are made to create energy

sewage (SOO-ij) the waste matter that passes through sewers

submersible (suhb-MUR-suh-buhl) a small ship capable of operating under water

tanneries (TAN-ur-eez) places where tanning or changing animal skins into leather takes place

FOR MORE INFORMATION

BOOKS

Dal Fuoco, Gina. *Rachel Carson: Renowned Marine Biologist and Environmentalist*. Minneapolis: Compass Point Books, 2009.

Fridell, Ron. *Protecting Earth's Water Supply*. Minneapolis: Lerner Publications, 2009.

Lasky, Kathryn. *John Muir: America's First Environmentalist*. Cambridge, MA: Candlewick Press, 2008.

Rooney, Frances. *Exceptional Women Environmentalists*. Toronto: Second Story Press, 2007.

WEB SITES

Environmental Kids Club
www.epa.gov/kids/
Information about how to help the environment and links to games and other fun activities

United Nations Environment Programme—TUNZA for Children
www.unep.org/Tunza/children/
Stories, facts, and activities to help you learn more about what kids can do to protect the environment

INDEX

ABOUT THE AUTHOR

Tamra B. Orr is a full-time author living in the beautiful Pacific Northwest. She has written more than 150 books for readers of all ages and learns something new every single time. She is mother to four and earned her degree from Ball State University. In her rare spare time, she likes to read, write old-fashioned letters, and visit the coast with her family.